Saskatchewan Handmade and Home-Based Listings 2018

4 Paws Games and Publishing

Bruno, SK

Saskatchewan Handmade and Home-Based Listings 2018

Compiled and written by 4 Paws Games and Publishing

Cover Art by 4 Paws Games and Publishing

Edited by 4 Paws Games and Publishing

Formatted and Published by 4 Paws Games and Publishing

First publication

Published July 2018

ISBN-13: 978-1-988345-80-2

Published by 4 Paws Games and Publishing

P.O. Box 444

Humboldt, Saskatchewan, Canada S0K 2A0

http://www.4-Paws-Games-and-Publishing.ca

TABLE OF CONTENTS

BIGGAR

Business Name: Voxx Life®

Name: Henrietta Parenteau

Address: Box 635, Biggar, SK S0K 0M0

Phone: (306) 948-6413

Email: henrietta.parenteau@sasktel.net

Products Sold: Voxx Life® Socks and insoles.

BRUNO

Artistic

Business Name: 4 Paws Games and Publishing

Name: Vickianne Caswell

Address: Box 444 Humboldt, SK S0K 2A0

Phone: (306) 290-0454

Email: Please message the page or website.

Website: www.4-Paws-Games-and-Publishing.ca

Social Media:
www.facebook.com/4.Paws.Games.and.Publishing

Products Sold: Books, series merchandise, author services, event planning, social media, and some website services, ECWID® store setup, photo videos, SK event advertising, image, and file conversions, and more.

Business Name: The Garage Gallery

Name: Robin Renneberg

Address: 429 Cheerie Street

Email: beyondthemomentdesigns@gmail.com

Website: www.thegaragegallerybruno.com

Social Media: www.facebook.com/thegaragegallerybruno

Products Sold: Saskatchewan artwork including, but not limited to paintings, sculptures, and jewellery.

Other

Business Name: 4 Paws Games and Publishing

Name: Vickianne Caswell

Address: Box 444 Humboldt, SK S0K 2A0

Phone: (306) 290-0454

Email: Please message the page or website.

Website: www.4-Paws-Games-and-Publishing.ca

Social Media:
www.facebook.com/4.Paws.Games.and.Publishing

Products Sold: Books, series merchandise, author services, event planning, social media, and some website services, ECWID® store setup, photo videos, SK event advertising, image, and file conversions, and more.

CRAVEN

Business Name: My Happy Snappy Jewellery

Name: Linda Gienow

Address: P.O. Box 23 Craven, SK S0G 0W0

Phone: (306)731-3619

Email: gienow90@gmail.com

Website: www.mymagnoliaandvine.ca/C863

Social Media: My Happy Snappy Jewellery on Facebook.

Products Sold: Magnolia and Vine®.

CUPAR

Handmade

Business Name: Saskatchewan Dachshund Club

Name: Dacie Matchett

Address: Box 189 Cupar, SK S0G 0Y0

Phone: (306) 450-9776

Email: saskdoxies@gmail.com

Website: www.saskdoxies.weebly.com

Social Media: Saskatchewan Dachshund Club on Facebook

Products Sold: Homemade items such as cups, pet treats, calendars, decals and more.

HARRIS

Handmade

Business Name: Saskgypsies

Name: Randy Cowan

Address: Box 276 Harris, SK S0L 1K0

Phone: (306) 260-7519

Email: crafty@saskgyspies.ca

Website: www.saskgypsies.ca/crafty

Social Media: www.facebook.com/Crafty-at-Saskgypsies-Jewellery-2108497079475962/

Products Sold: Jewellery made of copper with different textures, gems, minerals, and colours.

HERBERT

Direct Seller

Business Name: Love Apparel® by Kezia

Name: Kezia Menzies

Phone: 306-774-2192

Email: Kezijacks@hotmail.com

Products Sold: Clothing such as leggings, tops, dresses, and skirts. Willing to travel.

LIPTON

Business Name: Moni's Watkins

Name: Monica Knowles

Address: Box 184 Lipton, SK

Phone: (306) 336-2552 or (306) 331-8425

Email: uniquemonique_39@hotmail.com

Website: www.respectedhomeproducts.com/692990

Social Media: Moni's Watkins on Facebook.

Products Sold: J.R. Watkins®: Spices, personal products, ointments, salves, household products, dish soaps, cleaners, bathroom products, laundry products and candles.

MARTENSVILLE

Artistic

Business Name: Sprinkles the Clown

Name: Deseri Adrian

Address: Box 43 Martensville, SK S0K2T0

Phone: (780) 872-1288

Email: sprinklesclown@yahoo.ca

Website: http://sprinklestheclown.webs.com

Products Sold: Magic shows, walk around magic, balloon animals, mascots and strolling puppet shows.

MELFORT

Handmade

Business Name: Pillow Talk

Name: Wendy Hurd

Address: Box 3012 Melfort, SK S0E 1A0

Phone: (306) 921-9897

Email: pillowtalkwlh@gmail.com

Social Media: Pillow Talk on Facebook.

Products Sold: Unique, homemade pillowscapes to add a dramatic, decorative accent to any home, cabin, or workspace.

MIDDLE LAKE

Other

Business Name: Sunday Drive

Name: Andrea Carroll

Phone: (306) 231-9205

Website: www.sundaydrive.ca

Social Media: @sundaydrive.ca on Facebook

Services: Support shop local initiatives and community awareness through exposing niche markets (simpler even would be local owned business directory).

MOOSE JAW

Business Name: Magnolia and Vine®

Name: Denise Konieczny

Phone: (306) 631-7893

Email: mav.denise@shaw.ca

Website: www.mymagnoliaandvine.ca/c451

Social Media: www.facebook.com/snapstylebydenise

Products Sold: Snap-style customizable jewellery and interchangeable fashion accessories.

Business Name: TeaLife®

Name: Joanne Marta

Phone: (306) 313-8769

Email: joannestealife@gmail.com

Website: www.tealife.ca/biz/jmarta

Social Media: Facebook @Joannestealife

Products Sold: Quality loose leaf teas and accessories.

Business Name: Norwex®

Name: Edith Scholz

Phone: (306) 267-4400

Email: e.scholz@sasktel.net

Website: www.edithscholz.norwex.biz

Products Sold: Cleaning supplies without chemicals. Products for use in your home and in personal care.

Handmade

Business Name: Surrayah's Jewels

Name: Elaine Gill

Phone: (306) 693-4193

Email: e.gill@sasktel.net

Social Media: www.facebook.com/SurrayahsJewels

Products Sold: Hand-crafted jewellery and accessories specializing in seed bead weaving/bead embroidery, wire wrapping and hand painted pendants.

Other
Business Name: Woodrose and Sapphire Jewelelry

Name: Richelle Leptich

Phone: (306) 630-4946

Email: mamasvenue@gmail.com

Website: www.mamasvenue@gmail.com

Social Media: Woodrose and Sapphire Jewelry N' More on Facebook.

Products Sold: Bracelets, earrings, necklaces, rings, wine charms, bookmarks; with interchangeable gems that allow you to match your own style. Body jewellery; nose rings and navel rings.

RABBIT LAKE

Business Name: Puretrim® (Mediterranean Wellness)

Name: Doreen Lamb

Address: Box 37 Rabbit Lake, SK S0M 2L0

Phone: (306) 824-4450

Email: ddlamb@sasktel.net

Website: www.dlamb.puretrim.com

Social Media: N/A

Products Sold: Meal replacements, Boost tea®, Daily Complete vit's Experience®, Liver Master®, and Synergy Defense®. Puretrim Joint tea®, Pure Garden Skin Serum®, Joint Health Starter Pac®, 30-day weight loss challenge, 10-day weight loss challenge, and 30-day Liver master cleanse.

REGINA

Business Name: Elevacity®

Name: Tina Woronoski

Phone: (306) 539-3371

Email: elevate.tina@gmail.com

Website: https://elevacity.com/tinaleanne

Social Media:
https://www.facebook.com/groups/1921354694782852

Products Sold: Happy Coffee® and Xanthamax®.

Business Name: Terra Firma®

Name: Frank Boehm

Phone: (306) 530-3962

Email: frank.boehm@sasktel.net

Products Sold: Stone and crystal jewelry as well as diffuser bracelets.

Business Name: PRUVIT®

Name: Tess Boehm

Phone: (306) 529-2850

Email: pruvit@sasktel.net

Website: www.tessboehm.ShopKeto.com

Social Media: www.facebook.com/reginapruvit

Products Sold: Exogenous Ketones®, Keto Kreme® for Bulletproof Coffee®, and MCT oil.

Business Name: Elevacity®

Name: Frank Boehm

Phone: (306) 530-3962

Email: elevacity@sasktel.net

Website: www.elevacity.com/frankboehm

Social Media: www.facebook.com/elepreneurscanada

Products Sold: Smart Coffee®, Hot Chocolate, Keto Creamer®, "Happy Pills®," vitamin patches and weight loss coffee.

Business Name: Young Living®

Name: Tess Boehm

Phone: (306) 529-2850

Email: younglivingregina@sasktel.net

Website: www.youngliving.org/tessboehm

Social Media: www.facebook.com/younglivingregina

Products Sold: Oils, roller balls, healing crystals and more.

Handmade

Business Name: Kids N Kats – Sewing Creations

Name: Christine Euteneier

Email: kidsnkats@sasktel.net

Website: www.kidsnkats@sasktel.net

Social Media:
www.facebook.com/kidsnkatssewingcreations

Products Sold: Specializing in yoga props. Bolsters covered foam blocks, yoga straps, meditation cushions and sets, eye pillows, and yoga mat bags. A line of pillows and bags are available and custom orders for those unique products that can't be found on the market, are always welcome.

ROSTHERN

Handmade

Business Name: Fire Moon Soap Company

Name: Louisa Reddekopp

Address: P.O. Box 52, Rosthern, SK S0K 3R0

Phone: (306) 349-9420

Email: firemoonsoap@gmail.com

Social Media: Fire Moon Soap Co. on Facebook.

Products Sold: Handmade soaps, rose petal salve, lip balms, beard oil, Aloe Vera spray, smudge sprays, room, and linen sprays. Made with natural, locally sourced, organic ingredients whenever possible.

SASKATOON

Business Name: J.R. Watkins® by Lynnette Bates

Name: Lynnette Bates

Phone: (306) 203-1364

Email: lynnette@sasktel.net

Website: www.respectedhomebusiness.com/793223

Social Media: https://www.facebook.com/Watkins-by-Lynnette-Bates-922303274573432

Products Sold: J.R. Watkins®. Toilet bowl cleaner, all-purpose cleaners, and laundry soap. Gourmet: cinnamon, pepper, spices, vanillas, and extracts. Body care: lotions, salves, body washes, and soaps. Remedies: medicated ointment, liniments, and other products. The company has been around for 150 years.

Business Name: Seacret Direct®

Name: Bonnie Clemence

Phone: (306) 280-4917

Email: b.clemence@hotmail.com

Website: www.seacretdirect.com/bclemence

Social Media: Seacret® Skin for the Win – Bonnie Clemence on Facebook

Products Sold: Dead Sea mineral skincare, haircare, body care as well as nutrition.

Business Name: Stephanie's Totes and Home

Name: Stephanie Kelsey

Phone: (306) 270-8308

Email: stephanie-kelsey@hotmail.com

Website: www.mythirtyone.ca/skelsey

Social Media: Stephanie's Totes and Home Facebook group.

Products Sold: 31 Gifts®. Home storage and organization; travel accessories and luggage; purses; totes; wallets; home décor. Most products can be customized with names or icons.

Handmade
Business Name: Lalita

Name: Gladys Prentice

Phone: (306) 220-3831

Email: gfprentice59@gmail.com

Social Media: On Facebook.

Products Sold: Wedding and children's accessories.

Business Name: Handmade by LyLi

Name: Lynn Dufort and Linton Davenport

Phone: (306) 717-9094

Email: le.dufort@sasktel.net

Website: N/A

Social Media: Handmade by LyLi on Facebook.

Products Sold: Doll bunkbed/single bed with mattress and bedding. Doll receiving blankets, doll cradle with mattress, doll high chairs, children's car organizers, snap bags, colour again pillows, and children's shelf for Matchbox® cars or knickknacks. Microwave bowls, hair towels, thread and bobbin racks, ironing board extension cord holders, and Saskatchewan Roughrider coolers.

Business Name: Prairie Princess Bowtique

Email: prairieprincessbows@gmail.com

Social Media:
www.facebook.com/prairieprincessbowtique

Products Sold: Hair accessories such as headbands and hair clips made with a variety of materials. Newborn to adult sizes. Offering ready made items and custom orders.

Other

Business Name: L & L Business Services

Name: Lynn Dufort and Linton Davenport

Phone: (306) 717-9094

Email: le.dufort@sasktel.net

Website: N/A

Social Media: N/A

Products Sold: T1 Personal Tax services and T2 Corporate Tax services.

WEYBURN

Direct Seller

Business Name: Elavacity®

Name: Stephanie Loreth

Phone: (306) 891-4651

Email: weger_1@hotmail.com

Website: www.elevacity.com/StephanieLoreth

Social Media: Steph's New Adventures and Energized Way of Living Life page on Facebook.

Products Sold: Smart Coffee®: Columbian instant coffee which supports efforts to control appetite and enhance mental focus.

Xanthamax®: Supports well-being; Choclevate®: Delicious hot chocolate that supports efforts to control appetite and enhance mental focus; KetoCre®: Effective, delicious, and nutritious ketogenic creamer; Vitamin Patches®: Nutraceutical-based health in a patch. Energy, sleep, and hangover patches; Pure®: Removes heavy metals and toxins from body; Timeless®: Skincare for men and women; Elier Mud®: purifies and infuses skin with vital nutrients; and Elier Serum®: Control time and care for skin.

33

www.ingramcontent.com/pod-product-compliance
Lightning Source LLC
Chambersburg PA
CBHW060644030426
42337CB00018B/3440